Henry Ford

Jennifer Strand

abdopublishing.com

Published by Abdo Zoom™, PO Box 398166, Minneapolis, Minnesota 55439. Copyright © 2017 by Abdo Consulting Group, Inc. International copyrights reserved in all countries. No part of this book may be reproduced in any form without written permission from the publisher. Abdo Zoom™ is a trademark and logo of Abdo Consulting Group, Inc.

Printed in the United States of America, North Mankato, Minnesota
072016
092016

Cover Photo: Hatrsook/Library of Congress
Interior Photos: Hatrsook/Library of Congress, 1; North Wind Picture Archives, 4; Grogan Photo Company/Library of Congress, 5; James R. Martin/Shutterstock Images, 7; Dean Pennala/Shutterstock Images, 8–9; AP Images, 8, 11, 12, 17; George Grantham Bain Collection /Library of Congress, 10; Library of Congress, 13, 16, 18; Detroit Publishing Co/Library of Congress, 14–15, 19

Editor: Emily Temple
Series Designer: Madeline Berger
Art Direction: Dorothy Toth

Publisher's Cataloging-in-Publication Data
Names: Strand, Jennifer, author.
Title: Henry Ford / by Jennifer Strand.
Description: Minneapolis, MN : Abdo Zoom, [2017] | Series: Incredible inventors | Includes bibliographical references and index.
Identifiers: LCCN 2016941394 | ISBN 9781680792300 (lib. bdg.) | ISBN 9781680793987 (ebook) | 9781680794878 (Read-to-me ebook)
Subjects: LCSH: Ford, Henry, 1863-1947--Juvenile literature. | Automobile industry and trade--United States--Biography--Juvenile literature. | Industrialists--United States--Biography--Juvenile literature. | Automobile Engineers--United States--Biography--Juvenile literature.
Classification: DDC 338.7/6292/092 [B]--dc23
LC record available at http://lccn.loc.gov/2016941394

Table of Contents

Introduction

Henry Ford was an American **innovator**.

Ford did not invent the car.
But he made cars less expensive.

Early Life

Henry was born in 1863. He grew up on a farm. But he did not want to be a farmer.

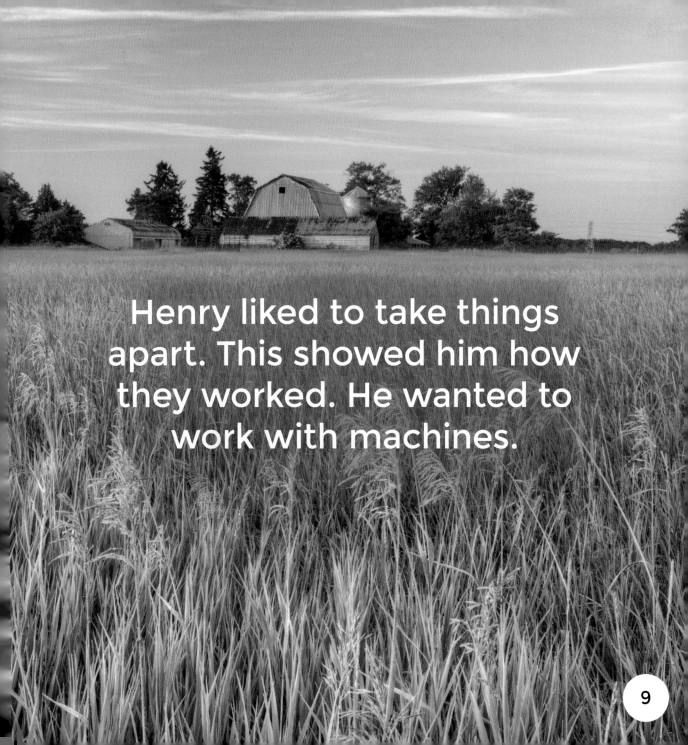

Henry liked to take things apart. This showed him how they worked. He wanted to work with machines.

9

Leader

Ford worked on making a car.

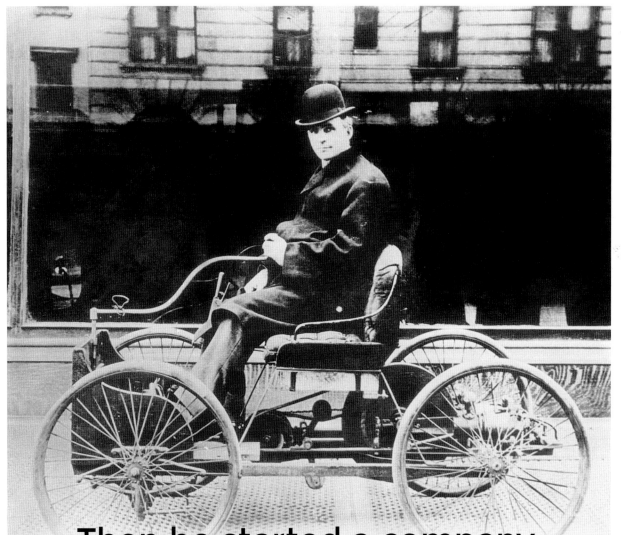

Then he started a company.
It made cars. His first big success
was called the Model N.

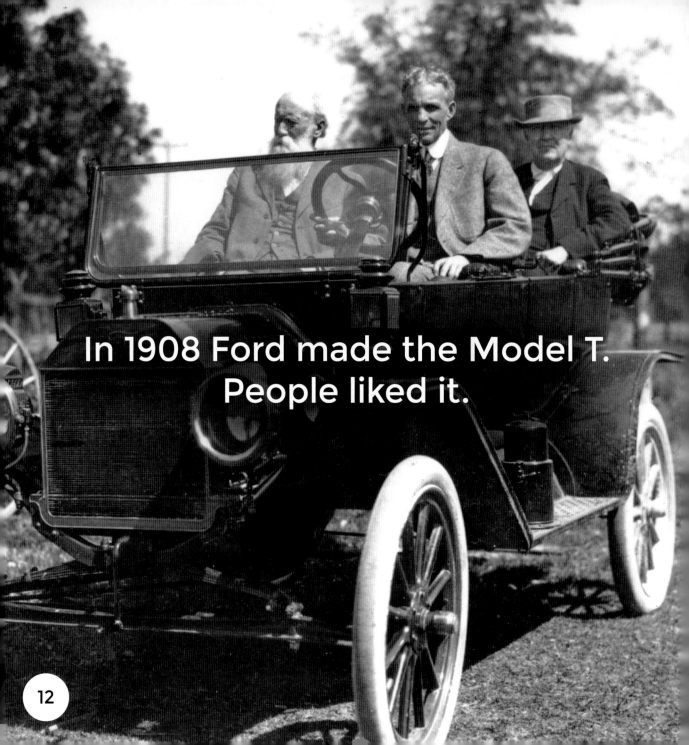

In 1908 Ford made the Model T. People liked it.

Soon it was the most **popular** car in the United States.

History Maker

At first one worker made the whole car. Then Ford opened a new factory.

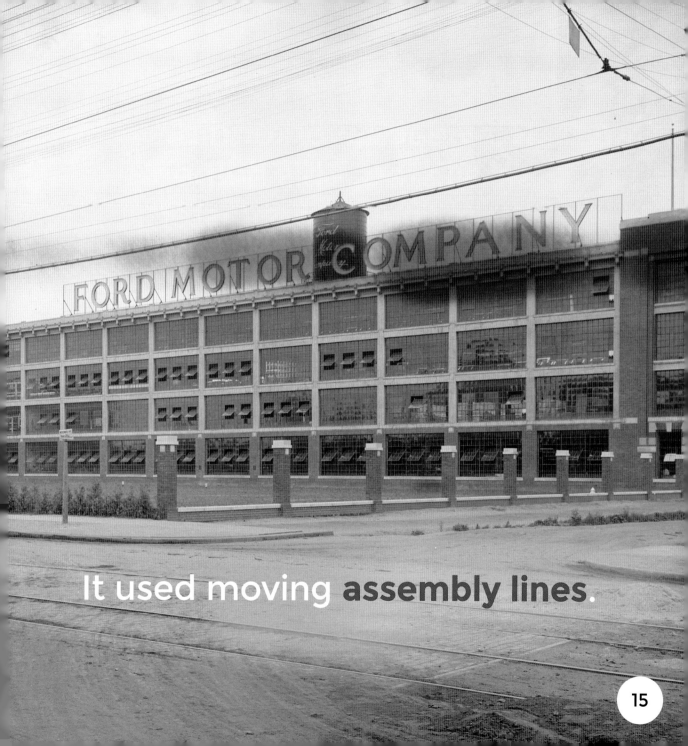

It used moving **assembly lines.**

Now each worker did a small step. This helped them make cars faster.

Ford's company was
very successful.

Legacy

Ford's ideas changed the way factories worked.

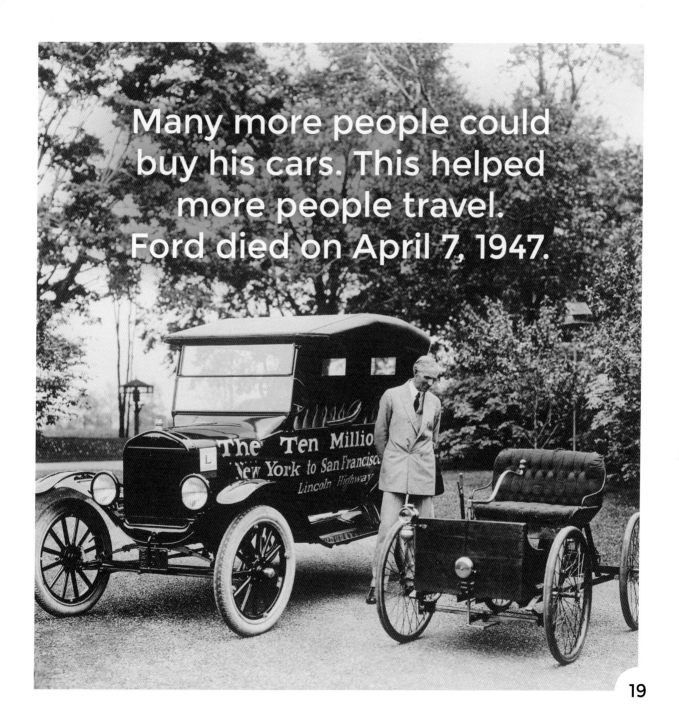

Many more people could buy his cars. This helped more people travel. Ford died on April 7, 1947.

Henry Ford

Born: July 30, 1863

Birthplace: Greenfield Township, Michigan

Wife: Clara Ala Bryant

Known For: Ford created the Ford Motor Company. His factories made cars cheaper and easier to build.

Died: April 7, 1947

#

1863: Henry Ford is born on July 30.

1896: Ford makes his first working car. It is called the Quadricycle.

1902: The Ford Motor Company is formed.

1908: Ford begins selling the Model T.

1913: Ford's new factory uses a moving assembly line.

1947: Ford dies on April 7.

Glossary

assembly line – a way of making something in which an item moves from worker to worker. Each worker does one step until the item is finished.

factory – a building where many products are made at one time.

innovator – someone who does something in a new way.

popular – liked or enjoyed by many people.

Booklinks

For more information
on **Henry Ford**, please visit
booklinks.abdopublishing.com

Z∞m In on Biographies!

Learn even more with the Abdo Zoom
Biographies database. Check out
abdozoom.com for more information.

Index